A Silent Scream For HELP

A Silent Scream For HELP

Understanding and embracing cultural differences
in learning environments

JUDY WATKINS

Illustrations by Randy Gray Illustrations
Louisville, Kentucky

gatekeeper press™
Tampa, Florida

A Silent Scream For Help
Understanding and embracing cultural differences in learning environments
Published by Gatekeeper Press
7853 Gunn Hwy, Suite 209
Tampa, FL 33626
www.GatekeeperPress.com

The cover design, interior formatting, typesetting, and editorial work for this book are entirely the product of the author. Gatekeeper Press did not participate in and is not responsible for any aspect of these elements.

Library of Congress Control Number: 2021931858

ISBN (paperback): 9781662907067
eISBN: 9781662907074

DEDICATION

This book is dedicated to my late father,
Joe Winters, aka, "Little Willie", a successful
businessman, humanitarian, revered mentor and
community leader who believed that education and
hard work were important, fundamental steps towards
self-sufficiency and success in life. He never failed
to ask, "Are you doing the very best you can?"

ACKNOWLEDGEMENTS

I am eternally grateful for my family, especially my grandchildren - Adaj, Jaden, Jada and Livie - and their peers who have first-hand experience as students and whose incredible insight helped me better understand their struggles, frustrations, anxieties and desire for change. I am so thankful and blessed for the never-ending support from my husband of 50 years, Sam. I sincerely appreciate my friends, colleagues, teachers, students, and parents who so willingly offered advice, opinions, suggestions and ideas for this project, and I am equally thankful for the many individuals who were subliminally helpful.

INTRODUCTION

Today teachers and students alike are struggling to excel in a broken educational system. While I believe the struggle can be overcome, I do wonder when the change is going to come. Meanwhile, too many students (number one customer in our educational system) are disillusioned about education, and a significant number of them are shaking their heads and simply giving up.

Have educators changed with the times enough to understand and play a significant role in developing our future leaders? Are we actively listening to students, asking them critical questions, and allowing them to openly express themselves? Are we exploring their value system and holding them accountable to it?

Who's leading them to believe that they will never be successful instead of encouraging them to pursue whatever they want to be? Are we supporting their participation in the development of their individual success plans and challenging them to honor their commitment to the plan? Are we making discovery and learning stimulating and fun for them?

Are students motivating themselves to learn and to clearly understand and appreciate the benefits and power of learning? Are they demonstrating mutual respect for teachers, parents, peers and their community? Are they committed to succeed in a complex and competitive world?

As parents, why aren't we more curious about why our children say they hate school? Are we engaging and exploring with their teachers and coordinating efforts to control or remedy situations before they loom out of control? Are we really listening to our children and following up with open-ended questions, or are we simply accepting a yes or no response? Are we talking through disagreements and working toward compromises rather than ignoring or giving them the silent treatment?

As a teacher I enjoyed learning from my students. My teaching days inspired me to pen my thoughts on what I believe is ideal and what I know is real when I think of schools and the institution of life-long learning.

This book does not intend to portray all teachers as people who don't care, that all parents don't pay attention or get involved, or that all students just co-exist in the classroom and do just enough to get by. On the contrary, I believe that most teachers care deeply about their students, and that they want the best for them; that most parents want their children to do better and go farther in life than they did; and that most students genuinely want to excel and be proud of their achievements. However, I do believe there are important missing pieces to these jobs we call caregiving, educating and learning. Yes, learning is wealth-building and a job that students should take seriously; and educating is a job that requires more critical thinking, facilitation, and negotiating skills.

There's a song I love listening to called *What About the Children* by Yolanda Adams. It reminds me of the days I spent in the classroom listening to hormone-raging teenagers who thought they knew everything, while I fought off the urge to scream out loud, but instead I had to constantly remind myself that I was once a teenager. I remember growing up when I had parents who expected me to be respectful and act like I had some sense or else. I knew better than to challenge the "or else". Unfortunately, the "or else" is challenged way too often in today's classrooms.

As a teacher, I wanted my students to know that I liked, cared for and respected them as young people. Second, it was important for me to clearly make an early impression that I was not afraid of being their teacher, and that I stood behind everything I said. Third, I demanded respect, and to honor our time together, I sought more buy-in by encouraging them to help create the classroom rules, best practices, and fun learning activities.

For example, during one of many negotiation sessions we agreed to a weekly talk show that would happen on Fridays on the condition that Monday through Thursday they, collectively, attend school satisfactorily, honor their fellow students and perform their class assignments to the best of their ability. The talk show provided a platform for them to open up and candidly express their opinions and concerns about things they would change given the opportunity. A normative culture was established, and the general consensus was that respect would always be a best practice, that it was okay to agree to disagree, and that facts should support beliefs.

It was my experience that this activity strengthened their leadership, speaking and listening skills, and it boosted their confidence and self-esteem. They discovered that their classroom was a "safe" place to explore and learn a lot about themselves - which made them think about attitude and behavior that could harm or benefit them in the long run. As such, they learned about each other, they bonded, empathized, supported, and held themselves and each other accountable.

I've never thought of students as "bad". I've always believed they were searching for their place in society. That's why I was always open to talking with them, actively listening to them, and genuinely showing them that I cared. This was time well-spent and worth its weight in gold.

There are various reasons why our educational system is failing our students, one of which was not a focus of this project (see Appendix). My primary motivation for writing the tidbits presented in *A Silent Scream For Help* was to encourage parents, students and educators to become a drum beat for systemic change in advancing a different kind of learning among teachers, students, care givers and educational leaders.

As you read, note the beginning section of each page reflects an ideal situation, the middle section reflects a real situation, while the last section provides food for thought, or perhaps a possible solution.

I hope *A Silent Scream For Help* makes you laugh out loud, and inspires parents, educators and students to continue searching for the way forward to make learning stimulating and cool, and ultimately begin mending a broken education system that has lasted way too long. Enjoy!

FOREWORD

This book is about a black youth, and indeed, all students who are trying to become engaged learners in a school system that does not understand the real value of culture, and far too many teachers who do not willingly accept responsibility for equity outcomes for all students. Like most students, Little Willie wants to be valued by his peers, teachers, and adult leaders around him, but often is overwhelmed with daily challenges of surviving and finding little refuge in the classroom. As a result, he is deeply confused and desperately wants his fair share of love and attention from caregivers in his life.

Authored by an educator who has taught students at primary and secondary educational levels as well as worked as a college administrator. Little Willie's struggles and lost opportunities, as evidenced in his educational experiences, are highlighted with powerful life-long learning, "truth-telling" communications and illustrations. This storytelling will resonate with readers who wish for a way forward for students, educators and systems that limit, in so many ways, equitable treatment in the lives of too many students.

M.B. Friend

My teacher helps motivate me to improve my comprehension.

"Ms. Teach said I should try reading a few minutes each day to improve my comprehension."

Allow them to read a few books that interest them in addition to the books required on the district's list, and they may not fall asleep reading.

My takeaway from class every day is worth its weight in gold.

Every student should be able to walk away from class with a clear understanding of the day's lesson.

Courtesy and respect are high on our list of class rules.

They might think twice about breaking the rules if they could help establish them. Yeah, it's called buy-in ... just saying.

My teacher shows respect and demands respect in return.

The adult can show cleavage, but the student can't sag or show underwear?

My teacher meets me where I am.

"Little Willie, your English scores from last year
are horrible. How did you get in my class?"

"Ma'am, it's called the electric slide.
... I just stepped, with all the other
students, right into your room!"

*Accept them where they are and help them develop a
learning plan based on what they did the previous year.*

Dad encourages me to show kindness.

"Little Willie, why were you in the counselor's office today?"

"Pops, I told that girl in my class that she hurt my freaking eyes!"

"Did she say anything about your beadie beads?"

Work on character building.

I feel safe in my classroom.

Teachers don't need to be armed; they need to teach. Students have enough stress about their safety on the streets.

My history teacher covers ALL American History.

"Little Willie, what have you learned in your history class about W.E.B. Du Bois?"

"Uh, well his name tells me that he must be the dude who managed Boyz II Men back in the day."

The importance and history of slavery must be included in the history books for students to gain knowledge of American History.

I am required to do something that will help me stay in a learning mode when I get in-school suspension.

"Little Willie, what are you working on during in-school suspension today?"

"Make no mistake, Ma'am ... I'm working on math ... yeah, countin' these Benjamins!"

If it's OK for students to do nothing in class, they will NOT disappoint!

My teacher never calls me a bad kid.

"Son, what classroom will you be in
today when I visit your school?"

"Just look for the room with the
'BeBe's Kids' sign on the door."

Is the kid bad, or is it the behavior that's bad?

My school prepares me
for conditions I will face
in the real world.

"Little Willie, you have the skills and GPA to be on the team, but you didn't make the cut for basketball because transportation may be an issue."

Can you trust and feel safe if fairness is missing?

My teacher rarely misses a day at work.

Will the real teacher please stand?

My teacher doesn't embarrass me; she helps me build self-esteem and confidence.

If this is the way to help build confidence and self-esteem, this student may be doomed.

My dad is committed to helping me succeed.

"Pops, do you think I should go out
for basketball this year?"

"Son, you're not good enough to play basketball."

Wow! Why didn't you just shoot him?

I'm able to maintain my individuality at school.

"Little Willie, why do you think it's OK
to dress like that for school?"

"Pops, if my signature look is lame,
they'll make fun of me."

Whatever happened to school uniforms?

My teacher appropriately and respectfully corrects me when necessary.

Try having a private conversation about sensitive matters instead of in front of the whole class.

My teacher consistently gives constructive feedback so I can improve.

"Here's your graded paper, Little Willie."

Show them the correct way, and chances are, they might get it right next time.

My counselor provides career and college exploration.

"Ms. Counselor, where's all that college and career information you promised me?"

"You can look for it in the cabinet over there."

Never let them beg for career and college information; it should always be readily available and accessible.

My school and family help prepare me for job readiness.

"How did your interview go today, son?"

"It was cool. I gave the interviewer a high five, said, 'Later, bruh,' on the way out, and he said, "Thank you very much; we'll call you.'"

How about a professional greeting and a firm handshake?

My teacher encourages collaboration, not competition, among students.

"Class, your individual science projects are due next week. The winner will be announced the following week."

They really need you to help them sharpen their interpersonal and collaboration skills while they're still developing, especially before they enter the real world.

I'm expected to go to school prepared and ready to learn every day.

"Little Willie, where's your homework?"

"Ma'am, my stupid pet thought it was dinner and ate it up!"

OK, Little Willie, bring your stupid pet to school tomorrow for show-and-tell."

Really? Honesty is the best practice.

I get tutored as needed without being made to feel like I'm stupid.

"Are they laughing at you, man?"
"Yeah, I was reading and Ms.
Teach *put me on blast."

"What did she say?"

"She said, "Little Willie, the word is
THE. It was THE yesterday. It is THE
today, and it will be THE tomorrow."

*Brain-shaming is the best way to make somebody
*go south.

I willingly take advice and direction from my teacher to do what will benefit me in the future.

"Little Willie, how do you plan on reaching your life's goals after you graduate?"

"Ma'am, right now I'm weighing what I know against what I've been told."

Students should not be told what they will never become. They need to be guided towards a career.

My teacher praises me for a job well done.

"Little Willie, you're definitely maintaining consistency on your math tests."

Look into the underlying reason(s) for a student's failing grades and consider whether or not the curriculum developed for the entire class can successfully accommodate a student who may be deficient in certain skill areas.

My teacher's actions illustrate her genuine care for students.

"Ms. Teach, can you spend a few minutes with me on math today?"

"No. You need to schedule an appointment with me."

Students might really need to feel loved by someone sometimes.

Parents are encouraged to get involved at my school.

PARENT INVOLVEMENT COMMITEE MEETING

TUESDAY
2:30-3:30 PM

PLEASE BE ON TIME FOR
ELECTION OF OFFICERS

Implement options that will encourage parent involvement when they can't get off work to physically attend school meetings.

I get special accommodations when necessary.

Remember to serve up some positive reinforcement to go along with that punishment.

My dad expects me to maintain the family tradition.

1.   Graduate
2.   Go to college
3.   Get a job
4.   Move out
5.   Don't call for money

Set high expectations, and then discuss them with your children at the dinner table.

My teacher encourages me
to continue my education
and stay motivated.

"Son, what movie do you have to watch
tonight for class tomorrow?"

"SCARED STRAIGHT ... again!"

*Teachers might understand their students' struggles
better if they would just take a little time to have some
candid one-on-one with them.*

My teacher shows strength and dependability.

"Pops, do you think my teacher will quit
in the middle of the school year?"

"I sure hope not, son."

Determine the real reason teachers miss so many days and find a solution.

My teacher encourages me to have the right attitude to be successful as a student and in the world of work.

"Little Willie, I need your homework."

"Naw, I'm good."

Help them find a reason to want to learn.

I learn more quickly and understand better because I can take schoolbooks home.

"Son, why do you bring your schoolbooks home if you never have homework?"

"Pops, the bugs can rest in these books instead of in my bed."

Motivate them by telling them that doing homework just might help them pick up some time management skills.

My teacher's hands-on approach helps me focus.

"Class, today in biology we're going
to dissect this alligator."

"OK. We ain't skeered."

Stimulation, focus, commitment and the desire to learn ... a recipe for student success.

My dad expects me to be in school every day.

"Why weren't you at school today, Little Willie?"

"Well, what had happened ... when I was praying this morning, I thought I heard a voice say it was Sunday."

Lying will get you nowhere. Break it on down with the truth.

It's obvious my teacher loves to teach.

"Students, I have to finish this report, so watch the video, answer the questions, and put your work on my desk on the way out."

Really? This job requires some serious energy, enthusiasm, and love of the work.

The boy's bathroom at my school is clean with ample urinals.

Caring about students includes caring about their health and safety.

My school understands the importance of transportation for students who participate in extracurricular activities.

"Pops, I have to stay after school
to practice soccer this week."

"Will the activity bus be dropping you off?"

"We don't have an activity bus, but you
could just send this car for me."

Maybe it's time to learn how to use public transportation.

My school understands me better because it is involved in my community.

Hey, what do you know about your students' neighborhoods?

I'm allowed to learn at my own pace.

"Little Willie, let me see your project
that's due in two days."

"OK ... I'm organizing my final
thoughts on that now."

Preparation is 50 percent of the challenge.

Food in the school cafeteria is nutritious and delicious.

"Hey, man, what's for lunch today?"

"A crap burger, some dead fries, and a chalk shake."

Could be his only meal of the day.

I'm required to master the different styles of writing in Language Arts before I can graduate.

"Class, the last paper you'll write before you graduate will be an autobiography."

Whose fault is it if, by your senior year, you don't know the difference between a biography and an autobiography?

My teacher encourages me to take ownership of my education.

"Little Willie, is this your work?"

"Yes ma'am, it's mine. Here's
my proof of ownership."

Only you can own the consequences of your actions.

My English teacher discusses with me the mistakes I make and shows me the correct way without insulting me or affecting my confidence.

"Little Willie, you can do better than this."

"Yes, ma'am, but what's wrong with it?"
"Just go to the board and write it
the correct way 100 times."
"OK!"

It only takes a few minutes — and a heart — to illustrate the correct way. If you don't, expect the same results next time.

My school helps prepare me for the challenges and responsibilities of adult life.

"Little Willie, you've been late to class three times this week. One more time and you get detention."

Is this what an employer would say to a consistently late employee? Help them learn accountability.

My teacher encourages me to participate in class.

"Class, I want to make sure each of you is fully engaged during class today."

"Why is your hand up, Little Willie? You g'tting' engaged?"

"Naw, fool, I ain't g'tting' engaged, I just want her to call on me!"

By all means, acknowledge the hand!

My school requires me to finish all required courses for the current school year during the current school year.

"Son, why are you doing junior English in the twelfth grade?"

"I didn't hear my teacher tell me to do this last year."

It's probably time for some hearing aids.

My teacher uses modern facilitation methods of teaching to make learning fun and interesting.

Allowing them to debate and have discussions might alleviate boredom.

My teacher sets appropriate limits.

"My teacher sent me to the nurse today because she thought I was having a seizure."

"What was wrong with you?"

"I was just chicken sleeping..."

Get off that cell phone at night, go to sleep and be prepared for class the next day. Leave that other action to the chickens.

My teacher speaks to me with respect.

R E S P E C T. Tell me what it means to you!

My teacher doesn't show favoritism.

"I got sent to the office again today."

"Why, son?"

"I had to *birth my food and my teacher
said I couldn't because another kid
had to go, but I went anyway."

*Sometimes getting in trouble is worth its weight in
something other than gold.*

My school promotes social and emotional learning.

"Hey pops, I'm keeping it a hundred this year."

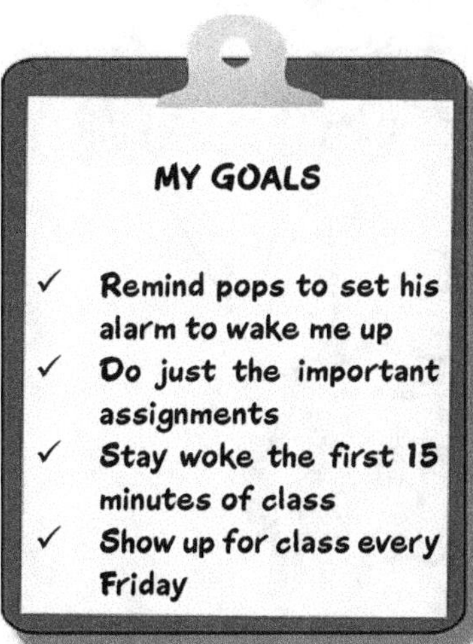

Develop a clear understanding of what setting realistic goals means.

My teacher's small-group facilitation makes me feel more confident and comfortable when openly expressing my thoughts.

"Little Willie, that really didn't make much sense."

Why keep kicking them when they're already down?

My teacher develops learning plans for me based on my personal and academic strengths and weaknesses.

"Little Willie, I don't recall which goals you achieved last year."

"I was in your class, Ms. Teach ... you don't remember me?"

"Uh, no ... but here's what I need from you this year if you intend to graduate."

No records from the previous year can hinder your ability to help them develop a plan for success in the current year.

My school makes the curriculum accessible for students and parents.

"Class, you and your parents can
view the curriculum online."

Don't assume every student has internet at home. Make paper copies of the documents and send them home with your students.

My school provides ample materials and supplies for all students.

"Son, why do you need all these supplies?"

"Pops, I'm my brother's keeper. Remember?"

STUDENT SUPPLIES LIST
10 writing tablets
100 #2 pencils
Headphones
100 ink pens w/eraser
SIM card
5 reams printing paper
Scientific calculator
20 pkgs loose-leaf paper
Field trip money
10 boxes of tissue

It's better to give than receive.

My teacher always explains new material to my understanding.

Would it be asking too much to use something they're interested in like math games, stock percentages or shooting pool, for example, to learn math?

When I'm not performing so well, my teacher finds a way to help me.

"Pops, Ms. Teach said I probably should consider moving to a class that's more on my level."

Clarity is important here. Exactly what does your "level" mean?

My teacher believes in me.

"Little Willie, do you believe you'll be able
to keep up a faster pace this year?"

"Ma'am, I believe I can fly."

*Get it right at your own pace if you want to run through
that open door!*

My school is a safe place for ALL students.

S O M E does not spell A L L.

My school has zero tolerance for racism and discrimination.

"Pops, a kid was dressed up like a KKK member for Halloween at school today."

"Did you tell someone?"
"Yeah. The principal said it was a clown costume meant to scare certain students."

This sounds like a case of "Somebody forgot to wear their glasses" or "Somebody misplaced the truth."

My teacher models the way we should handle conflict in a professional manner.

"OK, Little Willie, that doesn't sound accurate; let's hear the other side of the story."

Seems one-sided. Raise your hand if you think peer mediation might work better here.

Bullying is not allowed at my school.

"Why were you called to the
office today, Little Willie?"

"Dude said I was wearing a Folex and
Freeboks, so I kicked his butt."

A brand is just a name. Students must grow thicker skin or get busy learning how to create a brand of their own.

My school uses special dogs to sniff out alcohol and drugs.

"Son, what's the matter with you? Why were you sent home from school today?"

"My friends told me to try this new soda called Sodka because it's supposed to be so dope. I did and it made me sick."

Friends? Really? Stupid is as stupid does.

My dad encourages me to accept the differences of others.

"Dude, are we still on planet Earth?"

Beauty's only skin deep. Look for the positive in others.

My school provides monthly gun violence drills.

"Little Willie, when was your last gun violence drill at school?"

"The day after the last school shooting."

"What the heck? That was months ago!"

Never slack on something this important!

My dad expects me to do homework every night.

"Little Willie, what's your homework tonight?"

Uh ...

Parents may sometimes be old school, but don't play them for stupid.

My school prepares me for college.

"Little Willie, you probably should take that study skills class to improve your study habits in preparation for college."

"Naw, I'm good. I'll do exactly what I did here all four years ... read and study fifteen minutes every weekend."

Yeah, right; that's exactly why the sixth letter of the alphabet keeps taking center stage on those test papers.

My school won't promote me until I can prove mastery indicating college readiness.

"Little Willie, how did you do
on that science final?"

"I passed it."

Really? Somebody just made that up!

When I'm wrong, my teacher tells me privately.

"Little Willie, nobody wants to
see your underwear!"

"Ma'am, what you fail to realize is
that I'm wearing Gucci's."

Dude pull your pants up and put on a belt!

My classroom feels like a community — we support one another.

"Little Willie, your assignment is the only one that wasn't collected yesterday."

Yes, ma'am. I left it on the desk before leaving, but I guess the person who was supposed to be collecting the assignments didn't see it right here ON. THE DESK. IN THE FRONT ROW ... IN. BROAD. DAYLIGHT!

Turn it in yourself. Don't hold someone else accountable for your responsibilities.

I feel empowered in my classroom — knowledgeable, understanding of the rules, and trusting everyone will be compliant.

"Dude, you know you can't use your
cell phone in the classroom."

"What do you think my teacher
is doing over there?"

The school policy should apply to everyone.

My teacher doesn't spend our class time teaching to the test.

"Class, you have to learn this stuff!
State test time is fast approaching."

Try giving them mini quizzes regularly along the way to check for understanding.

My school adjusts the curriculum to address the unique needs of students.

"Class, this month we're going to be learning about different cultures and places you've visited."

How about learning about places, people, and things in their own communities?

My teacher doesn't insult my intelligence.

"Little Willie, can you spell DUI?"

"Yes ma'am, I sure can."
D E E. Y O U. E Y E."

Really? Lay off making insulting remarks.

APPENDIX

Identifying and Rectifying Behavioral Issues and
Learning Disabilities for Efficacy in Educating

Our nation's Public-School System cavity is not on the same page as our societal needs and demands. Mental health, behavioral issues and learning disabilities are at an all-time high, they are not being addressed, and solutions are not being strategically approached. We're so concerned that our youth are able to pass state benchmark exams, maneuver technologically, do homework and study on Chrome- books so much so that their learning patterns, habits, styles and needs are being neglected. Let alone their personal needs such as balanced meals, clean clothes, and hygiene, care givers to assist with homework, and teaching them manners and respect.

Never has there been so many cases of children on meds and "qualifying" for services such as IEPs, counseling (for behavioral and mental health) and Social Security Disability in and through our nation's public education system. We put them on meds and keep them in the same environment, knowing they could have a bad day or be affected by a color, a sound or an activity, yet we don't do anything beyond serving them pills.

I want to be part of the solution by establishing a school and programs that cater to students with "special needs" such as behavioral issues, because they have not received love and nurturing from a caregiver. This includes those who can't focus with an empty stomach, those who don't know to say yes/no, thank you/no thank you, please/may I, because they haven't been taught manners. I don't want to just pump students with toxic chemicals and/or shove them in a Special Education class and not give them the chance to learn, when they are capable. I agree that some need to be on meds, but I do not agree with those being categorized and filtered into classes where they aren't taught, but clearly have the ability to learn.

I believe we can make a difference through education and change our communities - one mind at a time.

Dr. Monique Brown
Dean of Adult Education
Atlanta Technical College
Atlanta, Georgia

INSPIRATION

Recently, I was moved by a video of a young man named Jeff Bliss from Duncanville, Texas, who allegedly returned to high school after dropping out. I was impressed by his decision to return to school, even as I listened closely to his heartfelt words about his frustration with the challenges he and his fellow students were experiencing in the classroom. Right click, or copy and paste link to watch https://youtu.be/bKjqjpePhTc

or read it here:

Jeff: *"Going off on kids cause they don't freakin get this crap?"*

Teacher keeps saying *"bye"* and *"get out"*

Jeff: *"If you would just get up and teach 'em instead of handing them a freaking packet, yo! There's kids in here who don't learn like that... They need to learn face to face. You're just getting mad because I'm pointing out the obvious."*

Teacher: *"No it's cuz you're wasting my time."*

Jeff: *"No I'm not wasting your time; I'm telling you what you need to do. You want kids to come into your class? You want them to get excited for this?"*

Jeff: *"You gotta come in here and make them excited. You want a kid to change and start doing better? You gotta touch his freakin heart. Can't expect a kid to change if all you do is just tell 'em."*

Teacher: "Bye"

Jeff: *You gotta take this job serious. This is the future of this nation. And when you come in here like you did last time and make a statement about 'oh this is my paycheck', indeed it is...but this and my country's future and my education. But there is a limit, when I'm not bitching, but simply making an observation. And now I will leave."*

"You're welcome! And if you like, I'll teach you a little more so you can actually learn how to teach a freaking class." (teacher keeps saying "bye" and "just go")

Jeff: "because since I got here, I've done nothing but read packets; so don't try to take credibility for teaching me jack."

Teacher: *"Close the door."*

And then the video cuts out.

I'm grateful for Jeff's observations and hope that his experience will help us better understand "what the heck is going on" with our students and that it will serve as a springboard to begin making substantial, essential changes to our educational system.

GLOSSARY

*fashiony slubby - inappropriately dressed woman

*shook - scared stiff

*chicken sleeping - head bobbing up and down while sleeping

*testing my gangsta - rocking my nerves

*birth my food - do the number 2

*talmbout - talking about

Be-Be's Kids – unruly kids (from the movie, "Be-Be's Kids")

*brain shaming - to make someone feel bad

*go south - to go bad

*put on blast - to embarrass

*From the Urban Dictionary